BOWS AND ARROWS

An Archery Bibliography

By

HOWARD BOBBS and MARCIA MUTH MILLER

THE SUNSTONE PRESS
Santa Fe, New Mexico / 1974

Most of the books listed in this
bibliography are in the personal
collection of Mr. Howard Bobbs.

The authors wish to express their
appreciation to Wm. Farrington
for his bibliographical assistance.

Printed in the United States of America

ISBN 0-913270-27-X

OF BOWS AND ARROWS AND BOOKS

One of the earliest and most important inventions of fledgling mankind was that of the bow. The bow and arrow changed man's history because it increased his ability to survive in what was often an hostile environment. And, because man himself has certain inherent tendencies toward aggression, it also increased his capacity to dominate others.

Whether used for good or evil, the bow and arrow became an integral part of expanding civilization until it was replaced by gunpowder. From the 15th century on, bows and arrows were gradually phased out as a principal source of weaponry and became instead a major sport. The popularity of archery was considerably enhanced by the fact that from the 13th century through the 19th century most of the ruling monarchs, the aristocracy and landed gentry in the various countries promoted it as a sport.

Today, archery is practiced both as a sport in itself and for hunting purposes. It is taught as a regular part of school physical education programs. There are many archery clubs and organizations. There are all kinds and varieties of tournaments. Archery was one of the 1972 Olympic events. First place winners in the men's and women's divisions, incidentally, were Americans.

From primitive man's necessity to modern man's pleasure has been a long evolutionary process. Perhaps today the growing popularity of archery can be attributed to the desire to get away (if only briefly) from the intensely technical and mechanical society in which we live.

Archery is a skill. It can be taught. It must be practiced and it requires a good eye and steady hands. It is a demanding art and this in part accounts for its popularity. Now when so much is done by turning a knob or switch, there is a great personal satisfaction to be gained from learning and using a skill which is so elemental.

Archers and archery have been a part of our myths, fables and litera-
ture since the introduction of the bow. Cock Robin, Cupid, Robin Hood and
William Tell are familiar to all children. Archery terms have been used for
descriptive purposes and to illustrate a point. Thus, we have such phrases as
"straight as an arrow" and "He has two strings to his bow."

Every enthusiast of an art or skill enjoys not only performing that art
or skill but also reading about it. He wants to read the history of it. He
wants to read suggestions and advice on how to improve his own performance
and he enjoys reading about other people who are doing this same art.

The collecting of books on a subject is a natural adjunct to performing
and reading. The archer wants to have more than just his personal knowledge, he wants to have at his side the accumulated knowledge and history of
all other archers. He wants to feel, through reading, that sense of his own
part in the long and honorable history of the bow and arrow.

Marcia Muth Miller

1.   ACKER, WILLIAM R. B. *The fundamentals of Japanese archery.* (Tokyo) 1937. 84p.

2.   *Arab archery.* tr. and ed. by Nabih Amin Faris and Robert Potter Elmer. Princeton, N.J.: Princeton University Press, 1945.

3.   *The archer.* v. 1, autumn 1951-   North Hollywood, Cal.

4.   *The archer's assistant, being an introduction to the art of shooting with the long bow, by a practical and ardent admirer of that noble pastyme.* New York: C.F.A. Hinrichs, 1856. 18p.
Extracts from *The young archer's assistant,* London, 1854, with the preface signed F. M.

5.   ARCHERS COMPANY. *Archers handbook.* Pinehurst, N.C.: The Company, n.d.

6.   *The archer's complete guide; or, Instructions for the use of the long bow.* By an expert. New York: Peck & Snyder, 1878. 26p.

7.   *The archer's guide.* By an old Toxophilite. London: T. Hurst, 1833. 178p.

8.   *The archers' magazine.* v. 1, July 1952-
Philadelphia.

9.   *The archer's manual; or, The art of shooting with the longbow, as practiced by the United Bowmen of Philadelphia.* Philadelphia: R. H. Hobson, 1830. 66p.

10.   *The archer's register,* 1864-1915. London: Howell, James & Co. 42 v. (ceased publication)

11.   *The archer's yearbook,* 1953 -   ed. by Patrick Clover. Fareham, Hants., Eng.: 1953 -

12.   *The archery.* New York: O. Judd, 1879. 30p.

13.   *Archery.* Bulletin no. 1, 1922-
Boston: National Archery Association of the United States of Am-
America.

14.   *Archery, a poem.* n.p.: Printed for the Author, 1793.
79, 54, 64p.

15.   *Archery; a sportsman's magazine devoted to hunting
& field.* v. 1, 1929-
Los Angeles: National Field Archery Association of the United
States of America.

16.   *Archery news.* v. 1-27, no. 6; Aug. 1922-Oct/Nov.,
1948. (ceased publication)

17.   *The archery review.* v. 1, Aug. 1931-   Tulsa, Okla.

18.   *Archery, riding guide.* 1954/56-
Washington: Division for Girls and Women's Sports of the American Association for Health, Physical Education and Recreation.

19.   *L'art d'archerie.* ed. by Henri Gallice. Paris:
Renouard, 1901. 29p. (see   #20)

20.   *The art of archery.* tr. by H. Walrond. Norristown,
Pa.: 1948. 29p. (see   #19)

21.   ARTON, KENNETH O. *Some bowyers notes.*
Gerrards Cross, Bucks., Eng.: The Author, 1953. 56p.

22.   ASCHAM, ROGER. *Toxophilus, 1545.* London:
Arber, 1868. 268p.

23.   _____. _____. ed. by Edward Arber. English
Reprints. Westminster: Constable, 1902.

24.   THE ATHLETIC INSTITUTE. *Archery.* Chicago:
n.d. 80p.

25. _____. *How to improve your archery.* Consultants: Eloise M. Jaeger and others. Chicago: 1962. 80p.

26. BARRETT, JEAN A. *Archery.* Pacific Palisades, Cal.: Goodyear, 1969. 88p.

27. *The basic technique of instinctive field shooting.* Redlands, Cal.: The National Field Archery Association, 1957 (?) 25p.

28. BAZIN, RENE. *The king of the archers.* tr. by Mary Russell. New York: Macmillan, 1934. 200p.

29. BEAR, FRED. *The archer's bible.* Garden City, N.Y.: Doubleday, 1968. 160p.

30. BERTIER, ALBERT DE, and others. *Le tir a l'arc.* Paris: Hachette, 1900. 407p.

31. BILSON, FRANK L. *English archery; handbook of the sport and guide to the making of equipment.* London: Covenanter Union, 1947. 33p.

32. _____. *Modern archery.* London: Paternoster Press, 1954. 63p.

33. BOY SCOUTS OF AMERICA. *Archery.* North Brunswick, N.J.: 1964. 36p.

34. BURKE, EDMUND. *Archery.* New York: Arco, 1961. 136p.

35. _____. *Archery handbook.* Greenwich, Conn.: Fawcett, 1954. 144p.

36. _____. _____. New York: Arco, 1954. 144p.

37. _____. *Field and target archery.* New York: Arco, 1961. 144p.

38.   ————. *The history of archery.* London: Heinemann, 1958. 232p.

39.   ————. ————. New York: Morrow, 1957. 224p.

40.   BUTLER, DAVID F. *The new archery.* New York: Barnes, 1968. 128p.

41.   BUTTS, HEBER. *Archery shooting technique.* (Seattle?) 1938. 83p.

42.   CAMPBELL, DONALD W. *Archery.* Englewood Cliffs, N.J.: Prentice-Hall, 1971. 76p.

43.   CANFIELD, JAMES WILLARD. *Handbook of archery terms, publications and records.* Albany, Ore.: F. Taylor, 1936. 56p.

44.   CLOVER, PATRICK. *The bowman's handbook.* Portsmouth, Eng.: 1954 (?) 92p.

45.   COLBY, C. B. *First bow and arrow.* New York: Coward-McCann, 1955. 48p.

46.   COOR, DONALD E. *The silver horn of Robin Hood.* Philadelphia: Winston, 1956. 238p.

47.   COSSON, ————; BARON DE. *The crossbow of Ulrich V, Count of Wurtemberg, 1460.* n.p.: 1892. 445-64p.

48.   COX, NICHOLAS. *The gentleman's recreation.* London: N. Rolls, 1697. 1v.

49.   CRAFT, DAVE, and CRAFT, CIA. *Teaching of archery.* New York: Barnes, 1936. 82p.

50.   DECKER, GEORGE C. *Bows and arrows for boys.* St. Paul: Bruce, 1930. 48p.

51.   DODD, JAMES WILLIAM. *Ballads of archery.* London: R. H. Evans, 1818. 175p.

52.   DOYLE, ARTHUR CONAN. *Sir Nigel.* New York: McClure, Phillips, 1906. 346p.

53.   _____. *The White Company.* New York: David McKay, 1958. 363p.

54.   DREYER, CARL. *Med bue og pil.* Copenhagen (?) S. Hasselbalchs, 1936. 291p.

55.   DUFF, JAMES, and MURRAY, MAY DUFF. *Archery poems.* ed. by C. N. Hickman. n.p.: Eastern Archery Association, 1956. 48p.

56.   DUFF, JAMES. *Bows and arrows.* New York: Macmillan, 1946. 173p.

57.   DUGUID, JULIAN. *Tiger-man.* London: V. Gollancz, 1932. 298p.

58.   EDINBURGH. ROYAL COMPANY OF ARCHERS. *Poems in English and Latin on Archers and Royal Company of Archers.* Edinburgh: 1726.

59.   _____. *A short history, the commendation of the Royal Archers, with a description of six of the Dukes of Scotland.* Written by the Tinklarian Doctor (W. Mitchel) Edinburgh: 1734.

60.   EDWARDS, CHARLES B. *An archer's notes.* Leeds, Eng.: Petty, 1949. 73p.

61.   EDWARDS, CHARLES B., and HEATH, E. G. *In pursuit of archery.* London: Kaye, 1962. 111p.

62.   ELMER, ROBERT P. *Archery.* Philadelphia: Penn Publishing Co., 1926. 456p.

63.   ELMER, ROBERT P., and SMART, CHARLES A., eds. *The book of the long bow*. Garden City, N.Y.: Doubleday, Doran, 1929. 207p.

64.   ELMER, ROBERT P. *Target archery*. London, New York: Hutchinson, 1952. 428p.

65.   FEATHERSTONE, DONALD F. *The bowman of England; the story of the English longbow*. New York: C. N. Potter, 1966. 200p.

66.   FISHER, RALPH A. *The guide to javelina*. San Antonio, Tex.: Naylor, 1951. 208p.

67.   FORBES, THOMAS A. *Guide to better archery*. Harrisburg, Pa.: Stackpole, 1955. 307p.

68.   _____. *New guide to better archery*. 2d ed., rev. & enl. Harrisburg, Pa.: Stackpole, 1960. 343p.

69.   FORD, HORACE A. *Archery, its theory and practice*. Cheltenham, England: J. Buchanan, 1856. 123p.

70.   FOY, TOM. *Beginner's guide to archery*. London: Pelham Books, 1972. 155p.

71.   FROBENIUS, LEO. *Morphology of the African bow-weapon*. New York: Stechert, 1932. 44p.

72.   GANNON, ROBERT. *The complete book of archery*. New York: Coward-McCann, 1964. 256p.

73.   GILLELAN, G. HOWARD, and STUMP, WILLIAM. *Archery handbook*. Los Angeles: Trend Books, 1958. 128p.

74.   GILLELAN, G. HOWARD. *Complete book of the bow and arrow*. Harrisburg, Pa.: Stackpole, 1971. 320p.

75.   _____. *Modern ABC's of bows and arrows*. Harrisburg, Pa.: Stackpole, 1967. 160p.

76. _____. *The young sportsman's guide to archery.* New York: Nelson, 1962. 96p.

77. GORDON, PAUL H. *The new archery.* New York: Appleton-Century, 1939. 423p.

78. GRIMLEY, GORDON. *Book of the bow.* Redlands, Cal.: National Field Archery Association, 1958. 242p.

79. GRISWOLD, LESTER E. *Handicraft; simplified procedure and projects.* 8th ed. Colorado Springs: The Author, 1942. 512p.

80. GROGAN, HIRAM J. *Modern bow hunting.* Harrisburg, Pa.: Stackpole, 1958. 163p.

81. GUTCH, JOHN M., ed. *A lytell geste of Robin Hode.* London: Longman, 1847. 2v.

82. HAMILTON, T. M. *Native American bows.* ed. by Nancy Bagby. York, Pa.: G. Shumway, 1972. 148p.

83. HANCOCK, H. J. B. *Archery.* The Bijou Book of Out-Door Amusements. n.p.: 1868. 89p.

84. *A handbook of archery.* Evansville, Ind.: The Indian Archery & Toy Corp., n.d. 8p.

85. *A handbook of archery.* San Francisco: Westmade Archery Tackle Co., 1932-33. 20p.

86. HANSARD, GEORGE AGAR. *The book of archery.* London: Henry G. Bohn, 1841. 456p.

87. HARE, KENNETH. *The archer's chronical and greenwood companion.* London: Williams & Norgate, 1929. 244p.

88. HARGROVE, A. E. *Anecdotes on archery.* York, Eng.: Hargrove's Library, 1845. 316p.

89.   HARRIMAN, MARGARET. *Bring me my bow.* London: Gollancz, 1967. 256p.

90.   HARRIS, PERCY VALENTINE. *The truth about Robin Hood.* London: 1954. 97p.

91.   HASTINGS, THOMAS. *The British archer.* Isle of Wight: The Author, 1831. 130p.

92.   HAUGEN, ARNOLD O., and METCALF, HARLEN G. *Field archery and bow hunting.* New York: Ronald, 1963. 213p.

93.   HAY, IAN. *The Royal Company of Archers.* Edinburgh: Blackwood, 1951. 299p.

94.   HAYNES, HENRY WILLIAMSON. *Bow and arrow unknown to palaeolithic man.* Proceedings, v.23. Boston: Society of Natural History, n.d.

95.   HEATH, ERNEST GERALD. *Archery; the modern approach.* London: Faber, 1966. 279p.

96.   _____. *Grey goose wing.* Reading, Eng.: Osprey Publications, 1971. 343p.

97.   HERRIGEL, EUGENE. *Zen, in the art of archery.* tr. by R. F. C. Hull. London: Routledge & Kegan Paul, 1953. 107p.

98.   HERTER, GEORGE L., and HOFMEISTER, RUSSEL. *Professional and amateur archery tournament and hunting instructions and encyclopedia.* Waseca, Minn.: Herter's, 1965. 228p.

99.   HILL, HOWARD. *The fine points of archery.* n.p.: Union Oil Company of California, 1958. 11p.

100.   _____. *Hunting the hard way.* English ed. London: Hale, n.d. 224p.

101. ———. ———. New York: Wilcox & Follett, 1953. 318p.

102. ———. *Wild adventure.* London: Hale, 1957. 223 p.

103. HOBBS, WILLIAM HERBERT. *Cruises along by-ways of the Pacific.* Boston: Stratford Co., 1923. 162p.

104. HOCHMAN, L. *The complete archery book.* New York: Arco, 1965. 144p.

105. HODGKIN, ADRIAN ELIOT. *The archer's craft.* London: Faber and Faber, 1951. 222p.

106. ———. ———. New York: Barnes, 1961. 222p.

107. HOOGERHYDE, RUSS, and THOMPSON, C. G. *Archery aims; archery as a sport, with common sense shooting methods.* Bristol, Conn.: Archers Company, 1933. 54p.

108. HOUGHAM, PAUL. *The encyclopedia of archery.* New York: Barnes, 1958. 202p.

109. ———. *Hit that target.* (Tulare, Cal.) 1954. 55p.

110. HOYLE, EDMOND. *Hoyles games.* New and correct ed. London: Jeffery, 1843. 165p.

111. HUNT, W. BEN, and METZ, JOHN J. *The flat bow.* Milwaukee: Bruce, 1936. 70p.

112. *Individual sports for women.* 4th ed., ed. by Dorothy S. Ainsworth. Philadelphia: Saunders, 1963. 326p.

113. INTERNATIONAL CONGRESS OF AMERICANISTS, RIO DE JANEIRO, 1922. *Annaes do XX Congresso Internacional de Americanistas.* v.1 Rio De Janeiro: 1924. 436p.

114.   JAEGER, ELOISE M. *Archery.* New York: Sterling, 1961. 128p.

115.   KLANN, MARGARET L. *Target archery.* Reading, Mass.: Addison-Wesley, 1970. 162p.

116.   KLOPSTEG, PAUL. *Turkish archer and the composite bow.* Evanston, Ill.: The Author, 1947. 187p.

117.   KROEBER, ALFRED LOUIS. *Arrow release distribution.* Publications in American Archaeology and Ethnology, v.23, no.4. Berkeley: University of California, 1927.

118.   KROEBER, THEODORA. *Ishi.* Berkeley: University of California Press, 1961. 258p.

119.   KUESTER, LILLIAN LORETTA. *Archery manual; a practical guide for instructors and novices.* South Hadley, Mass.: The Author, 1928. 32p.

120.   LACOMBE, PAUL. *Arms and armour in antiquity and the middle ages.* tr. by Charles Boutell. London: Reeves & Turner, 1907. 296p.

121.   LAMBERT, ARTHUR W. *Modern archery.* New York: Barnes, 1929. 306p.

122.   LAYCOCK, GEORGE, and BAUER, E. A. *Hunting with bow and arrow.* New York: Arco, 1966. 111p.

123.   LEWIS, JACK P., ed. *Bow and arrow archer's digest.* Northfield, Ill.: Digest Books, 1971. 320p.

124.   LONGMAN, C. J., and WALROND, H. *Archery.* Badminton Library. London: Longmans, Green, 1894. 590p.

125.   LOVE, ALBERT J. *Field archery technique.* Corpus Christi, Tex.: Dotson Printing Co., 1956. 121p.

126.   MCEVOY, HARRY, JR. *Archery today.* Oak Park, Ill.: Broadhead, 1937. 63p.

127.   MACHEN, ARTHUR. *The bowmen and other legends of the war.* London: Simpkin, Marshall, Hamilton, Kent, 1915. 86p.

128.   MCKINNEY, WAYNE C. *Archery.* 2d ed. Physical Education Activities series. Dubuque, Iowa: W. C. Brown, 1971. 58p.

129.   MANDEL, JOSEPH D. *Archery workshop.* New York York: The Author, 1952. 62p.

130.   MARKHAM, GERVASE. *The art of archerie.* 1634. Reprint. York, Pa.: G. Shumway, n.d.

131.   MASON, OTIS T. *North American bows, arrows and quivers.* Washington, D.C.: U.S. National Museum, 1889 (?) 162p.

132.   MASON, RICHARD OSWALD. *Use of the long bow with the pike.* Intro. by Stephen V. Grancsay. facsim. York, Pa.: G. Shumway, 1970. 59p.

133.   MAXSON, LOUIS W., comp. *Spalding official archery guide.* New ed., rev. by Edward B. Weston. New York: American Sports Publishers, 1910. 130p.

134.   MEYER, HERRMANN. *Bogen and Pfeil in Central-Brasilien.* Ethnographische Studie. Leipzig: 1895. 54p.

135.   MORGAN, THOMAS C. *The devil's post office.* London: Hutchinson, 1955. 224p.

136.   MORSE, EDWARD S. *Additional notes on arrow release.* Salem, Mass.: Peabody Museum, 1922.

137.   _____. *Ancient and modern methods of arrow-release.* Bulletin of the Essex Institute, vol. xvii, Oct.-Dec., 1885. Salem, Mass.: 1885. 56p.

138. ⸻. *On the so-called bow-pullers of antiquity.* Bulletin of the Essex Institute, vol. xxvi, 1894. Salem, Mass.: 1894. p.141-66.

MUIR, JOHN, pseud. see MORGAN, THOMAS C.

139. MURDOCH, JOHN. *Study of the Eskimo bows in the U.S. National Museum.* Washington, D.C.: U.S. National Museum. 1884.

140. NASU, TOSHISUKE. *Japanese archery.* tr. by William R. B. Acker. New ed. Rutland, Vt.: Tuttle; Englewood Cliffs, N.J.: Prentice-Hall, 1965. 84p.

141. NATIONAL FIELD ARCHERS ASSOCIATION OF THE UNITED STATES, INC. *Bowhunting manual.* 2d ed. Redlands, Cal.: 1962. 176p.

142. ⸻. *Official handbook of field archery.* 10th ed. Redlands, Cal.: 1959. 151p.

143. NEADE, WILLIAM. *The double-armed man.* York, Pa.: G. Shumway, 1971. 51p.

144. *The New Zealand archery handbook.* n.p.: The New Zealand Archery Association, Inc., 1956. 140p.

145. NIEMEYER, ROY K. *Beginning archery.* Rev. ed. Belmont, Cal.: Wadsworth, 1967. 56p.

146. PARKER, CLEMENT C. *Compendium of works on archery.* Philadelphia: McManus, 1951. 74p.

147. PAUL, JAMES BALFOUR. *The history of the Royal Company of Archers, the Queen's bodyguard for Scotland.* Edinburgh: Blackwood, 1875. 394p.

148. PAYNE-GALLWEY, Sir RALPH W. F. *The crossbow.* New York: Bramhall House, 1958. 329p.

149. _____. *A summary of the history, construction and effects of warfare of the projectile-throwing engines of the ancients, with a treatise on the structure, power and management of Turkish and other oriental bows of medieval and later times.* London: Longmans, Green, 1907. 44, 26p.

150. PEACHMAN, HARRY. *The compleat gentleman.* 3d impression. London: E. Tyler, 1661.

151. PERRY, WALTER. *Bucks and bows.* Harrisburg, Pa.: Stackpole, 1953. 223p.

152. POPE, SAXTON T. *The adventurous bowman.* New York: Putnam, 1926. 233p.

153. _____. *Bows and arrows.* Foreword by Robert F. Heizer. Berkeley: University of California Press, 1962. 83p. Originally published in 1923 with title: *A study of bows and arrows.*

154. _____. *Hunting with the bow and arrow.* San Francisco, Barry, 1923. 245p.

155. _____. *Yahi archery.* Publications in American Archaeology and Ethnology, v.13, no.3. Berkeley: University of California, 1918.

156. POWNALL, C. *Archery records, together with an introductory chapter and notes and reminiscences.* Woking, Eng.: G. F. Falls, 1929. 18p.

157. PSZCZOLA, LORRAINE. *Archery.* Philadelphia: Saunders, 1971. 107p.

158. RAUSING, GAD. *The bow; some notes on its origin and development.* Acta Archaeologica Lundensia. Ser. in 8°, no. 6. Lund, Sweden: Gleerup, 1967. 189p.

159.   REICHART, NATALIE, and KEASEY, GILMAN. *Archery.* New York: Barnes, 1936. 132p.

160.   _____. _____. 3d ed. New York: Ronald, 1961. 78p.

161.   RHODE, ROBERT J., comp. *Archery champions.* Minneapolis: The Compiler, 1960. 212p.

162. RICHARDSON, MARGHERITA EMILY. *Archery.* London: Teach Yourself Books, 1970. 127p.

163;   _____. *Teach yourself archery.* London: English Universities Press, 1961. 127p.

164.   ROBERTS, DANIEL. *Archery for all.* New York: Drake, 1971. 160p.

165.   ROBERTS, THOMAS. *The English bowman; or tracts on archery.* London: The Author, 1801. 296p.

166.   *Robin Hood, English outlaw.* London: Longman, Hurst, 1820. 240p.

167.   ROTH, BERNHARD A. *Archery.* New York: Putnam, 1962. 128p.

168.   ROUNSEVELLE, PHILLIP. *Archery simplified.* New York: Barnes, 1931. 120p.

169.   _____. *Student's handbook of archery; for all beginning archers.* New York: Barnes, 1932. 64p.

170.   ROYAL TOXOPHILITE SOCIETY, LONDON. *A history of the Royal Toxophilite Society.* Taunton: H. Abraham, 1867. 125p.

171.   RUSHTON, WILLIAM L. *Shakespear, an archer.* London: Truslove & Hanson, 1897. 118p.

172.   SCHMIDT, MARVIN T. *Introduction to archery.* Chicago: Ziff-Davis, 1946. 110p.

173.   SCHUYLER, KEITH C. *Archery, from golds to big game.* South Brunswick: Barnes, 1970. 569p.

174.   SHANE, ADOLPH. *Archery tackle.* Peoria, Ill.: Mancel Arts Press, 1936. 112p.

175.   SIEMEL, SASHA. *Tigrero!* New York: Prentice-Hall, 1953. 296p.

176.   SIGLER, HOWARD T. *Pocket field guide to archery.* Harrisburg, Pa.: Stackpole, 1960. 96p.

177.   SLAUGHTER, FRANCES E., ed. *Archery.* The Sportswoman's Library. London: A. Constable, 1898. 49p.

178.   SMITH, DONNAN R. *Hand book on archery.* 2d ed. San Francisco: California By-products Co., 1926. 32p.

179.   SOLLIER, ANDRE, and GYORBIRO, ZSOLT. *Japanese archery; Zen in action.* New York: Walker & Co., 1970. 94p.

180.   SPENCER, STANLEY FARWELL. *Spencer system of shooting the bow.* San Pedro, Cal.: The Author, 1933. 100p.

181.   STALKER, TRACY L. *How to make modern archery tackle.* n.p.: The Author, 1954. 37p.

182.   STAMP, DON. *The challenge of archery.* Buffalo, N.Y.: Black Academy Press, 1971. 151p.

183.   STEIN, HENRI. *Archers d'autre fois; archers d'aujourd'hui.* Paris: Longuet, 1925. 305p.

184.   STEMMLER, LOUIS EDWARD. *Archery workshop.* 3d ed. Queens Village, N.Y.: The Author, 1935. 103p.

185. _____. *Essentials of archery; how to use and make bows and arrows.* Queens Village, N.Y.: L. E. Stemmler Co., 1937. 92p.

186. STRUTT, JOSEPH. *Sports and pastimes of the people of England.* New ed. London: T. Tegg, 1831. 420p.

187. SULLIVAN, GEORGE. *Better archery for boys and girls.* New York: Dodd, 1970. 64p.

188. SUMPTION, DOROTHY. *Archery for beginners.* Philadelphia: Saunders, 1932. 141p.

189. TAYBUGHA, fl. 1368. *Saracen archery; an English version and exposition of a Mameluke work on archery (ca. A. D. 1368)* With an introd., glossary and illus. by J. D. Latham and W. F. Paterson. London: Holland Press, 1970. 219p.

190. TEMPERLEY, CLIVE. *Shooting at the blazon.* London: Straker, 1938. 8p.

191. THOMPSON, MAURICE. *My winter garden.* New York: Century, 1900. 302p.

192. _____. *Songs of fair weather.* Boston: J. R. Osgood, 1883. 99p.

193. _____. *Sylvan secrets in bird songs and books.* New York: J. B. Alden, 1887. 139p.

194. _____. *The witchery of archery.* New York: Scribner, 1878. 259p.

195. _____. _____. ed. by Robert P. Elmer. Pinehurst ed. Pinehurst, N.C.: The Archers Co., 1928. 259p.

196. THOMPSON, WILL H. *How to train in archery.* New York: E. I. Horseman, 1879.

197.   TREGEAR, E. *Polynesian bow.* Washington, D.C.: Smithsonian Institution, 1893.

198.   WALROND, H., ed. *The archer's register, 1909-1910.* London: Horace Cox, 1910. 302p.

199.   ⸺. *Archery for beginners.* London: Horace Cox, 1905. 31p.

200.   WAMBOLD, HOMER R. *Bowhunting for deer.* Harrisburg, Pa.: Stackpole, 1964. 160p.

201.   WARING, THOMAS. *A treatise on archery or the art of shooting the long bow.* London: The Author, 1827. 67p.

202.   ⸺. ⸺. 7th ed. London: T. Waring, 1828. 62p.

203.   WATSON, JOHN BROADUS, and LASHLEY,

203.   WATSON, JOHN BROADUS, and LASHLEY, KARL SPENCER. *The acquisition of skill in archery.* Papers from the Department of Marine Biology. Washington, D.C.: Carnegie Institution, 1915.

204.   *What the beginner needs to know about archery.* London: Slazenger Archery Equipment Co., n.d. 13p.

205.   WHIFFIN, LAURENCE C. *Shooting the bow.* Milwaukee: Bruce, 1946. 83p.

206.   WHITE, STEWART EDWARD. *Lions in the path; a book of adventure on the high veldt.* New York: Doubleday, 1926. 292p.

207.   WILBUR, C. MARTIN. *The history of the crossbow.* Smithsonian Institution, Annual Report, 1936. Washington, D.C.: 1937. p.427-38.

208.   WISEMAN, HOWARD, and BRUNDLE, FRED. *Archery*. London: W. & G. Foyle, 1956. 112p.

209.   _____. and _____. *Archery from A-Z*. London: Faber, 1958. 127p.

210.   WISEMAN, HOWARD. *Tackle archery this way*. London: Stanley Paul, 1959. 128p.

211.   WOOD, WILLIAM. *The bowman's glory; or, Archery revived*. New preface by E. G. Heath. 1682. facsim. of 1st ed. London: Society of Archer-Antiquaries and the Grand National Archery Society, 1969. 85p.

HOWARD BOBBS — A native of Pennsylvania has lived in New Mexico since 1939. In 1940, he opened an art gallery and studio in Santa Fe. He is the sixth generation of artists in his family and has achieved national prominence as a painter of the landscape and people of New Mexico. Archery itself as well as the history of archery has long been a hobby with Mr. Bobbs.

MARCIA MUTH MILLER — A librarian and free-lance writer, she is a graduate of the University of Michigan.

www.ingramcontent.com/pod-product-compliance
Lightning Source LLC
LaVergne TN
LVHW091238080426
835509LV00009B/1326